IT'S TIME TO EAT ORGANIC GELATIN

It's Time to Eat ORGANIC GELATIN

Walter the Educator

Silent King Books
A WhichHead Entertainment Imprint

Copyright © 2024 by Walter the Educator

All rights reserved. No part of this book may be reproduced in any manner whatsoever without written per- mission except in the case of brief quotations embodied in critical articles and reviews.

First Printing, 2024

Disclaimer

This book is a literary work; the story is not about specific persons, locations, situations, and/or circumstances unless mentioned in a historical context. Any resemblance to real persons, locations, situations, and/or circumstances is coincidental. This book is for entertainment and informational purposes only. The author and publisher offer this information without warranties expressed or implied. No matter the grounds, neither the author nor the publisher will be accountable for any losses, injuries, or other damages caused by the reader's use of this book. The use of this book acknowledges an understanding and acceptance of this disclaimer.

It's Time to Eat ORGANIC GELATIN is a collectible early learning book by Walter the Educator suitable for all ages belonging to Walter the Educator's Time to Eat Book Series. Collect more books at WaltertheEducator.com

USE THE EXTRA SPACE TO TAKE NOTES AND DOCUMENT YOUR MEMORIES

ORGANIC GELATIN

It's time to eat, hooray, hooray,

It's Time to Eat
Organic Gelatin

A yummy treat to brighten our day.

Wiggly, jiggly, oh so fun,

Organic gelatin for everyone!

Made with fruits so fresh and sweet,

A healthy snack we love to eat.

Mango, berry, apple delight,

Each little bite feels just so right.

No colors fake, no sugar too,

Just wholesome things are good for you!

It sparkles bright in shades so clear,

A special treat to bring us cheer.

Grab a spoon and scoop it high,

Watch it wiggle, wave, and fly!

It's like a dance upon your plate,

A squishy jig we celebrate.

It's Time to Eat Organic Gelatin

Parents smile and say, "Oh my,

This treat is good, come give it a try!"

It's made with care, so pure and clean,

The best dessert you've ever seen!

Little bears or circles round,

Gelatin shapes are fun to be found.

Stars and hearts, or wobbly cubes,

A rainbow of snacks that lift your mood.

It's easy to make, let's try it now,

Mix and stir, we'll show you how.

Add some juice, then let it set,

A wiggly surprise we won't forget!

When snack time comes, we clap and cheer,

Our jiggly treat is finally here!

Organic gelatin, soft and sweet,

It's Time to Eat

Organic Gelatin

A tasty way to have a treat.

So grab a bowl, enjoy the fun,

Healthy snacks for everyone!

Organic gelatin, pure delight,

A wiggly hug in every bite.

Hooray for treats that wiggle and shine,

It's Time to Eat

Organic Gelatin

It's time to eat, let's all dine!

ABOUT THE CREATOR

Walter the Educator is one of the pseudonyms for Walter Anderson. Formally educated in Chemistry, Business, and Education, he is an educator, an author, a diverse entrepreneur, and he is the son of a disabled war veteran. "Walter the Educator" shares his time between educating and creating. He holds interests and owns several creative projects that entertain, enlighten, enhance, and educate, hoping to inspire and motivate you. Follow, find new works, and stay up to date with Walter the Educator™

at WaltertheEducator.com

www.ingramcontent.com/pod-product-compliance
Lightning Source LLC
LaVergne TN
LVHW010413070526
838199LV00064B/5288